# BITE ME, I'M COLORING

### DE-STRESS WITH 50 HILARIOUSLY FUN SWEAR WORD COLORING PAGES

By John Brueckner

Illustrations by Joey Carolino

DARE YOU

STAMP CO.

A belligerent subset of
Cider Mill Press Book Publishers

CIDER MILL
PRESS

BOOK
PUBLISHERS

KENNEBUNKPORT, MAINE

13-Digit ISBN: 978-1-60433-724-2
10-Digit ISBN: 1-60433-724-9

This book may be ordered by mail from the publisher. Please include $5.99 for postage and handling. Please support your local bookseller first!

Books published by Cider Mill Press Book Publishers are available at special discounts for bulk purchases in the United States by corporations, institutions, and other organizations. For more information, please contact the publisher.

Cider Mill Press Book Publishers
"Where good books are ready for press"
PO Box 454
12 Spring Street
Kennebunkport, Maine 04046

Visit us online!
www.cidermillpress.com

Typography: Adobe Garamond, Archive Tilt,
Festivo Letters, Satisfy, and Typography of Coop

Printed in China
5 6 7 8 9 0

**DARE YOU**

**STAMP CO.**

If you've gotten this far, then you're our kind of asshole! Or perhaps you're already a fan of our little Dare You Stamp Company that's long been producing irreverent products that support voicing the rebellious chord in each of us.

Whether you've used our Bite Me Stamp Kit on that denied insurance claim, or sent your egotistical ex one of our "You Suck" postcards, you know we firmly believe in free speech, free expression, and especially the inalienable right not to be fucked with when we're coloring!

Color any number of these wildly "expressive" pages until everyone else calms the hell down or at least learns better than to disturb you when you're working on your masterpiece! And if they don't, well then, color any number of the following pages and leave your handiwork on that annoying colleague's desk, that shit-for-brains roommate's bed, or on the windshield of that driver who took up two parking spaces. Even if your world is running smoothly, and you couldn't be happier, think of the laughter your friends will have when you send them a hand-colored page that says "Not My Circus, Not My Monkeys!" If you run out of coloring pages in this book, check out *Fuck Off, I'm Coloring* for even more swear word fun. In fact, if you're a true badass, tag your art on social media with #BiteMeImColoring and get the recognition you've always desired! Hell, we even double-dog DARE you!

# SHARE YOUR BADASS MASTERPIECES

As you fill in each colorful phrase, don't keep it to yourself—let the good feelings fly! Snap a pic, add the hashtag #BiteMeImColoring, and tag us on social media (@cidermillpress)—we can't wait to climb aboard your rage train and enjoy the ride!

# INDEX

# TABLE *of* CONTENTS

# INTRODUCTION

Stressed out? Frustrated? Pissed off? We've got you covered... or rather, colored. We all know that the act of coloring unleashes some serious meditative power—putting colorful pen to intricately-designed paper has been calming us down since we were kiddos. So why not get back to basics and add in a little grown-up twist: colorful language. Combine the calming act of coloring with the satisfaction of throwing around a good strong swear word, and feel your tension dissipate!

We've created swear-word coloring pages perfect for any situation that makes you want to let loose a string of curse words, from crappy co-workers to annoying exes, with phrases like Shitbird and Couldn't Give a Shiny Shit. We've even created some awesome "Winning at Life" coloring pages that let you unleash your inner badass by adding some color to phrases like Fan-Fucking-Tastic and Living the Dream.

So, rather than screaming "Bite Me!" from your cubicle and risking that dreaded visit to HR, take our approach to calming down—grab a marker, flip to any page, and let loose! Everyone else can just back off because, well, you're coloring!

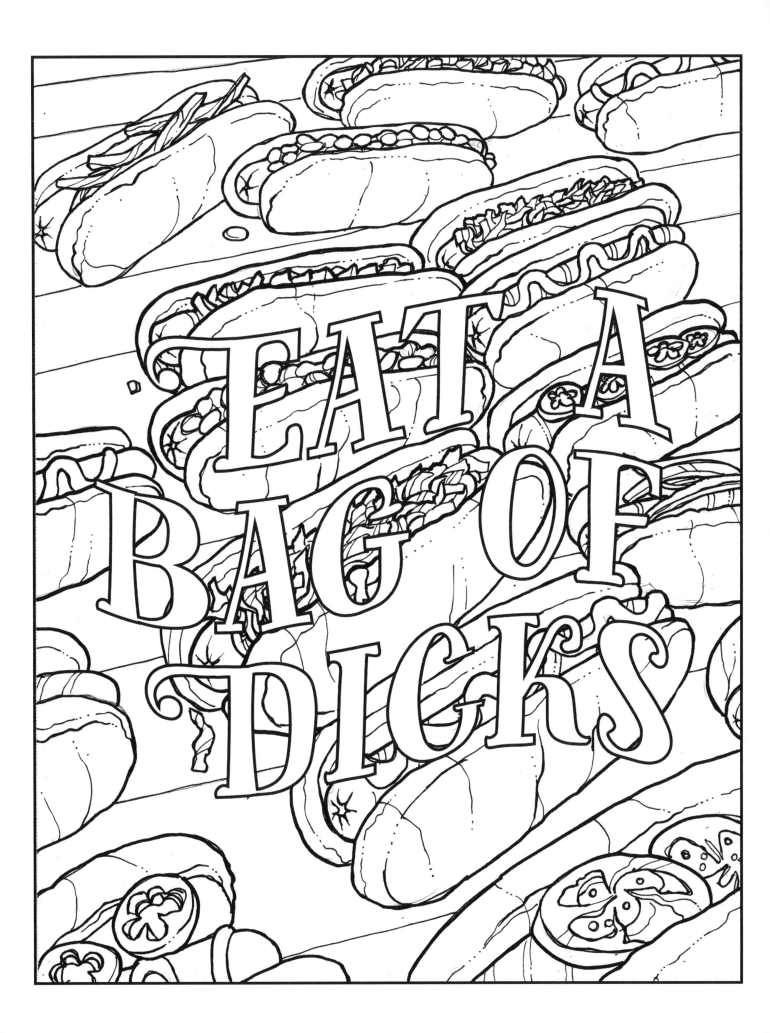

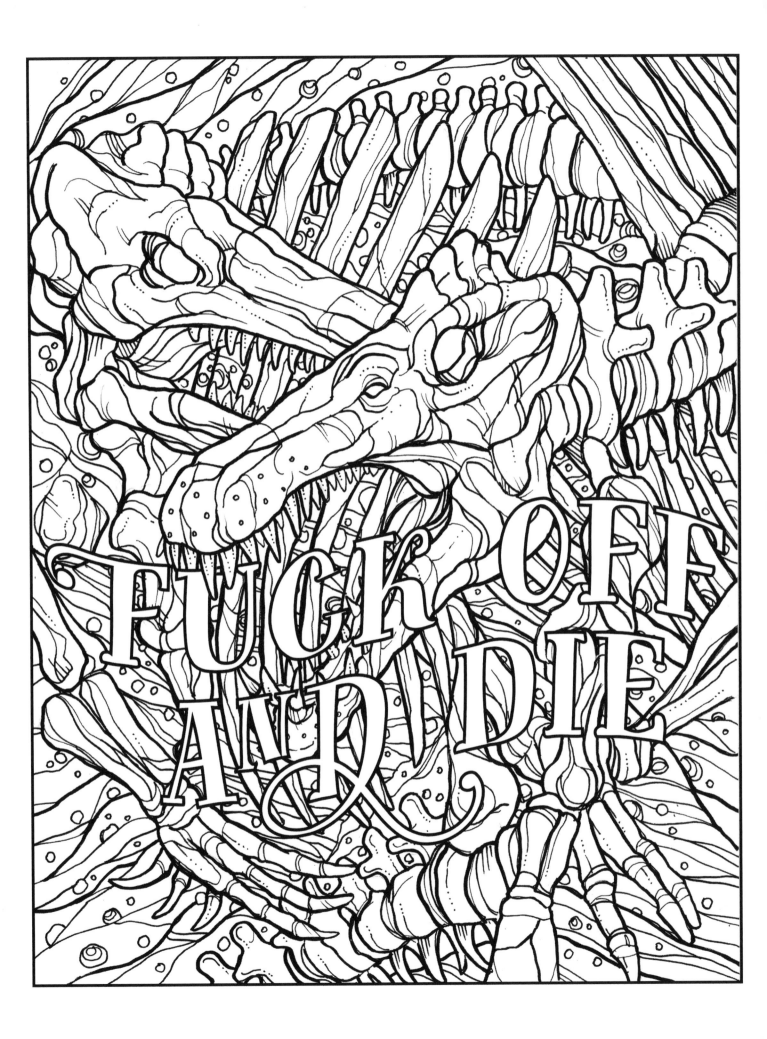

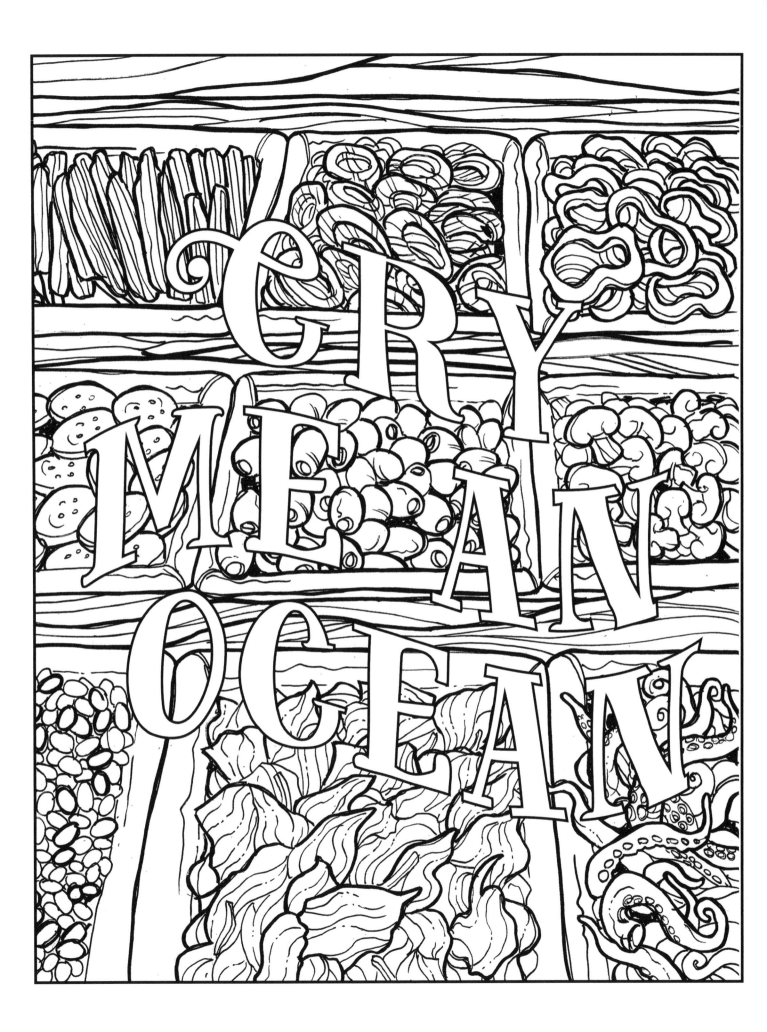

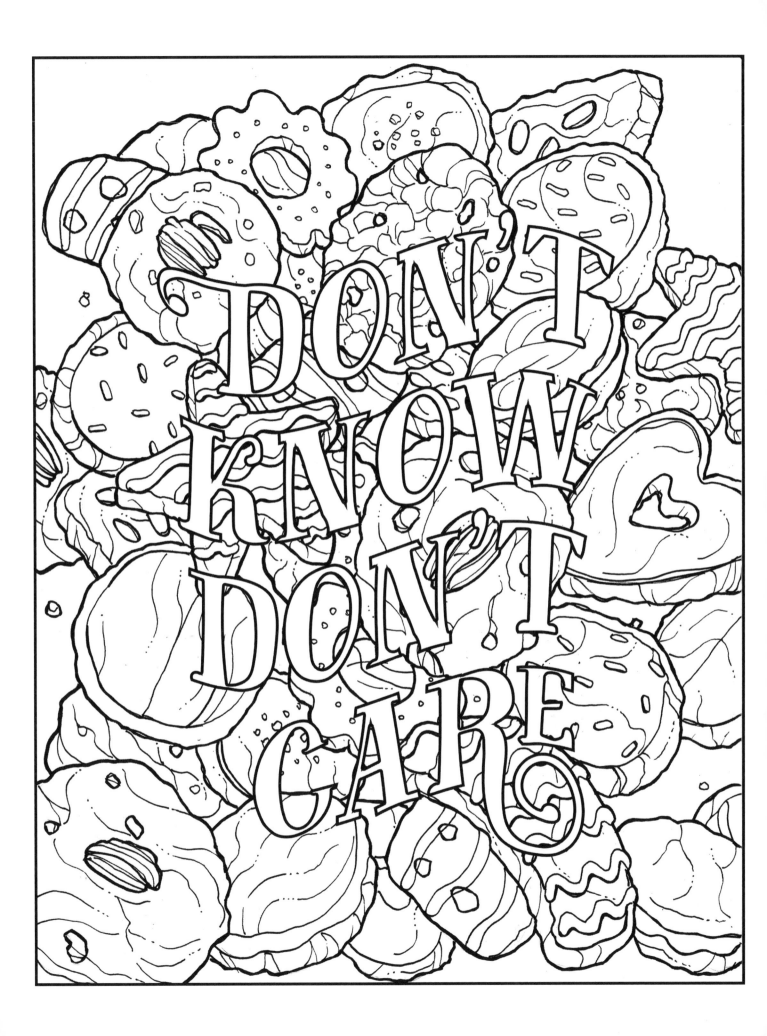

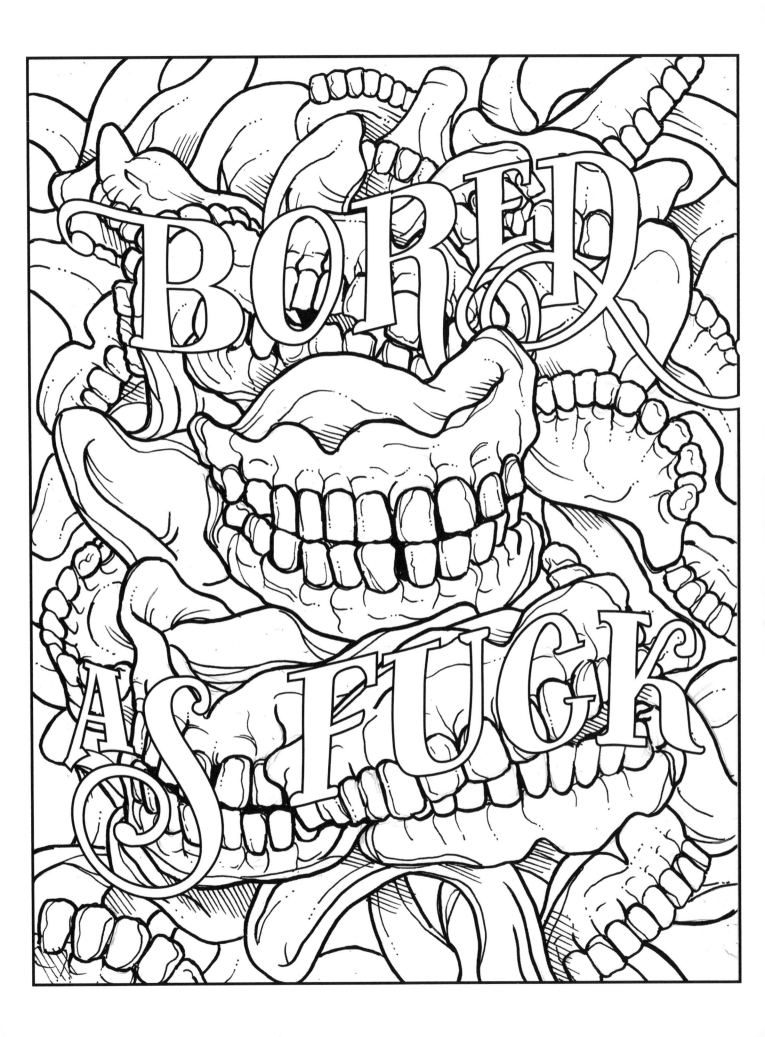

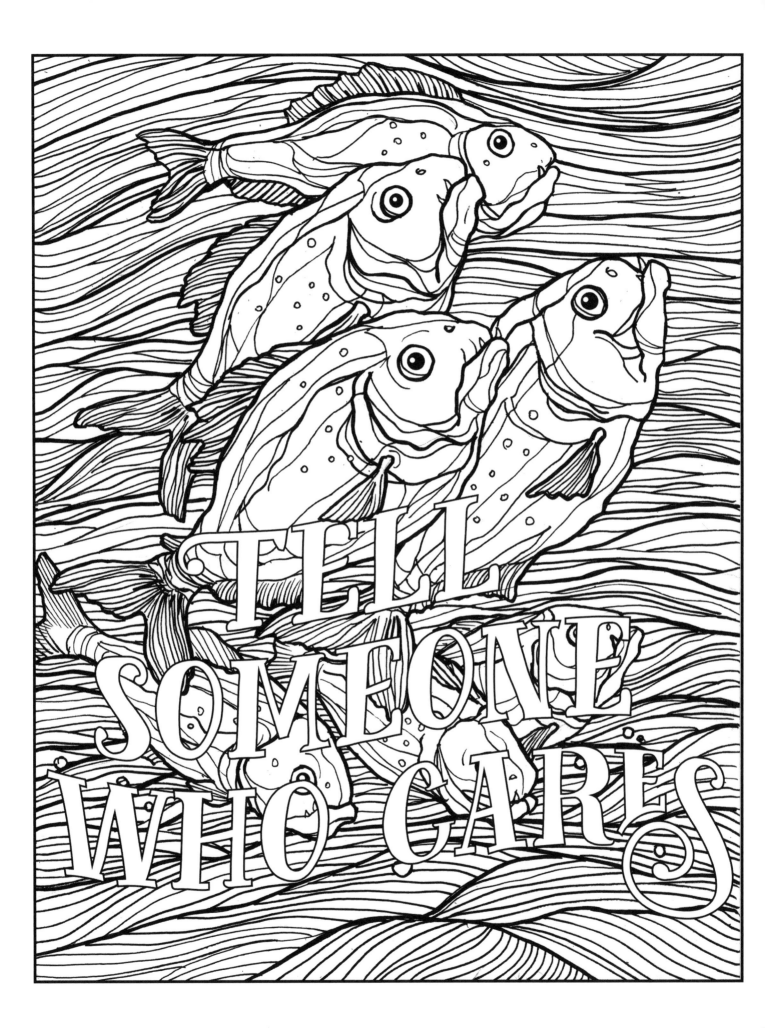

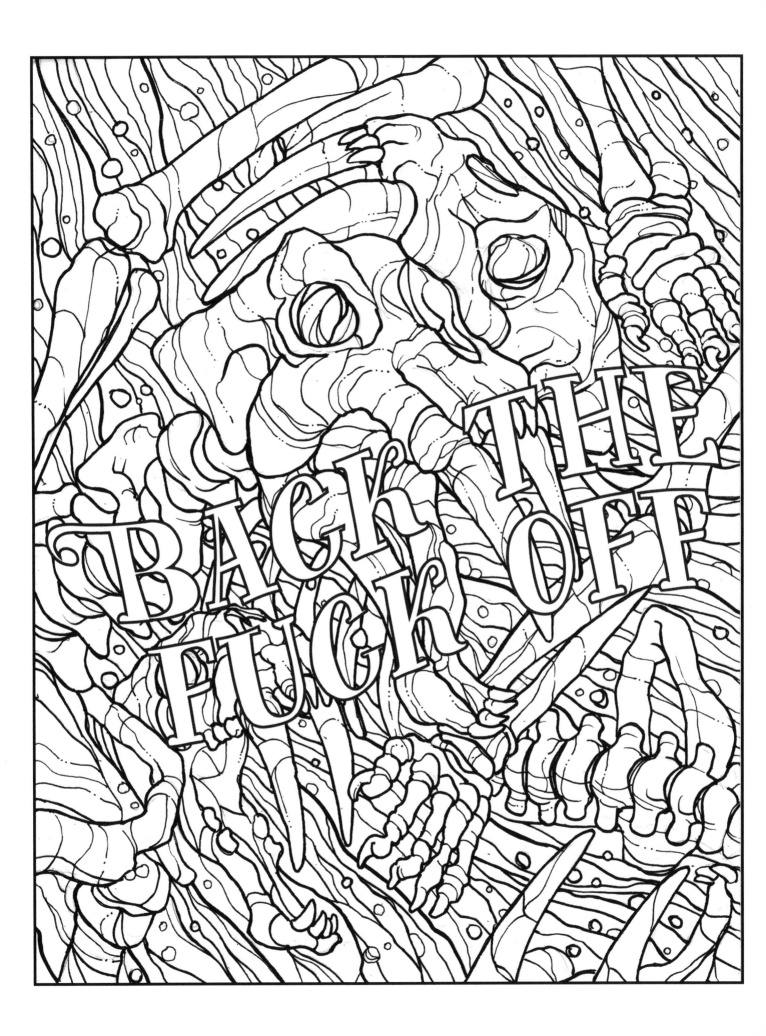

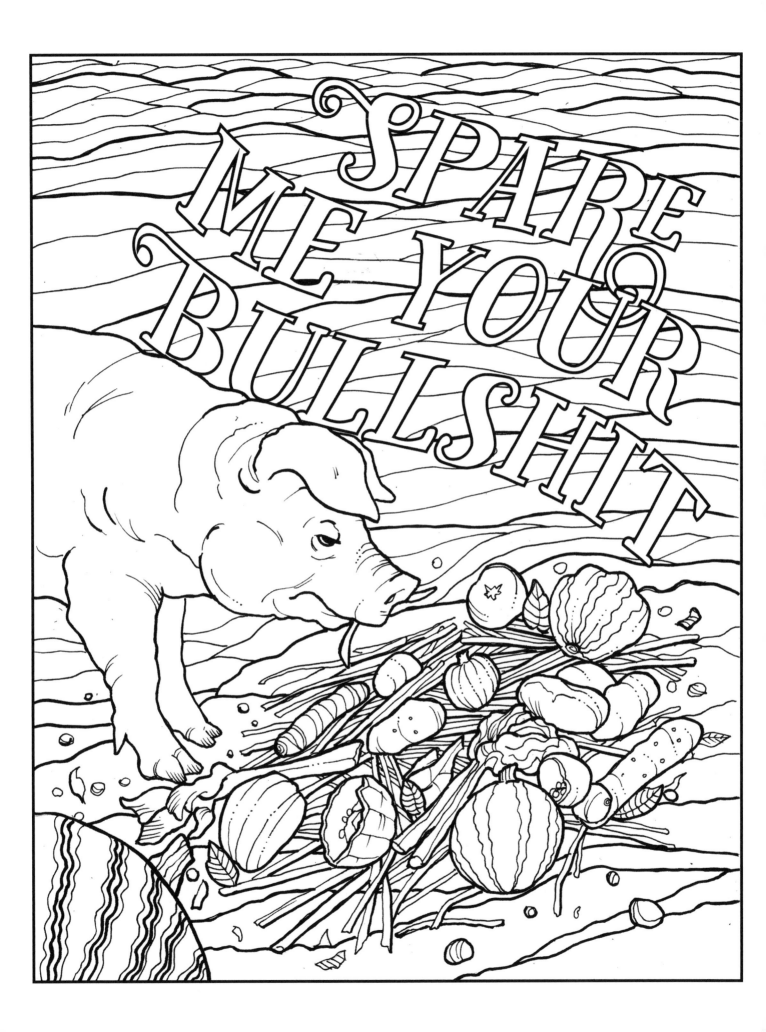